THE
LOOKING
GLASS

ISABELLA
GARDNER

THE LOOKING GLASS

NEW POEMS

THE UNIVERSITY OF CHICAGO PRESS

Library of Congress Catalog Card Number: 61-15932

THE UNIVERSITY OF CHICAGO PRESS, CHICAGO & LONDON
The University of Toronto Press, Toronto 5, Canada

© *1961 by The University of Chicago. Published 1961. Composed and printed by*
THE UNIVERSITY OF CHICAGO PRESS, *Chicago, Illinois, U.S.A.*

For Rose Van Kirk
and Daniel Seymour

These poems first appeared in the following magazines:

The Atlantic Monthly
CANZONETTA
SUMMER REMEMBERED

Beloit Poetry Journal
SUMMERS AGO

Chicago Choice
A PART OF THE DARK

Chicago Review
SALOON SUITE
ZEI GESUND

Hudson Review
LETTER FROM SLOUGH POND

Minnesota Review
THE SEARCHLIGHT
A LOUD SONG MOTHER

Mutiny
LITTLE ROCK ARKANSAS 1957
IN MEMORY OF LEMUEL AYERS

Poetry
THE WIDOW'S YARD
AND THOU NO BREATH AT ALL

Prairie Schooner
MEA CULPA

The New Republic
THAT PRINCELING
MATHEMATICS OF ENCOUNTER

The New Yorker
AT A SUMMER HOTEL

Sewanee Review
NIGHTMARE
THE LOOKING GLASS

Texas Quarterly
WRITING POETRY
NOT AT ALL WHAT ONE IS USED TO

The translations from *Jean Sans Terre*, by Yvan Goll,
are reprinted by permission of the publisher, Thomas
Yuseloff, Publisher; copyright 1958 by Claire Goll.

CONTENTS

NIGHTMARE

A sleeping woman dreams she wakes
Into a surging room of shrieks
and shapes. In the frantic room a red
haired woman looms . . . on her bent arm
there sleeps a girl's carved wooden head
A doll-sized nursing bottle nipples her huge palm.
Both head and bottle drop and leeringly she
beckons. The dreamer screams her hatred
of the leering shape. Scrabbling for safety
the dreamer flounders on the floor.
The leerer pounces from behind the door.
The struggling dreamer stands
The dreamer lifts and clenches both her hands
The dreamer rips the red curls
in handfuls from that hateful head and hurls
the hairy gobbets at those manic eyes
The leerer dreadfully diminishes in size
She shrinks and shrinks into a little child.
The screaming dreamer beats the dwindling child.
The dreamer lifts a chair to smash that leering child.
Nothing at all remains. Not hag nor child.
No traces and no tokens.
The red-haired dreamer wakens.

THE WIDOW'S YARD

"Snails lead slow idyllic lives" . . .
The rose and the laurel leaves
in the raw young widow's yard
were littered with silver. Hard-
ly a leaf lacked the decimal scale
of the self of a snail. Frail
in friendship I observed with care
these creatures (meaning to spare
the widow's vulnerable eyes
the hurting pity in my gaze).

Snails, I said, are tender skinned.
Excess in nature . . . sun rain wind
are killers. To save themselves
snails shrink to shelter in their shells
where they wait safe and patient
until the elements are gent-
ler. And do they not have other foes?
the widow asked. Turtles crows
foxes rats, I replied, and canned
heat that picnickers aband-
on. Also parasites invade
their flesh and alien eggs are laid
inside their skins. Their mating
too is perilous. The meeting
turns their faces blue with bliss
and consummation of this
absolute embrace is so
extravagantly slow
in coming that love begun
at dawn may end in fatal sun.

The widow told me that her
husband knew snails' ways and his garden had been Eden for them. He
said the timid snail could lift three
times his weight straight up and haul
a wagon toy loaded with a whole
two hundred times his body's burden.
Then as we left the garden
she said that at the first faint chill
the first premonition of fall
the snails go straight to earth . . . excrete
the lime with which they then secrete
the opening in their shells . . . and wait for spring.
It is those little doors which sing,
she said, when they are boiled.
She smiled at me when I recoiled.

ZEI GESUND*

For Dr. Louis Cholden
1918–1956

In the preposterous sunlight
we watched them wincingly lower you
into your formal April grave.
In strict tears they tolled the Hebrew
litanies which (though you were not pious)
had wailed in the ark of your ear
and blown in the shule of your heart
as remindingly as Shofar.
You lived your life and died your death by
love, and if on that spring day you could
have spoken from the upholstered
isolation of your coffin, you would
have taken to yourself the sorrow
of your uncountable bereaved,
as you did always, possibly saying "that
I am the reason you are grieved
and that I cannot rouse to laugh you out
of tears distresses me as dying
can no longer." Louis, it is true
that when those loved do die our crying
is made most difficult to suffer
by the unstoppable sharing
of what we imagine to have been
the die-er's panic and despairing
in this ultimate encounter.
You spared us that pain, for knowing
your life-spirit robust past compare
we knew that you had braved your going
with your accustomed curiosity

* *Zei Gesund* is a Yiddish phrase meaning literally "Be well"; it is used in leave-taking; therefore: "Farewell." *Shule* is the Jewish word for temple; *shofar*, for the ram's horn blown on the Day of Judgment.

and calm and courage. Every tear
is for ourselves, for our own loss,
the forever absence of you. Were
Death a hag (like those dishevelled
ladies in asylums whom you re-
deemed to dignity through your
accepting word and touch) I do be-
lieve you would have lent Ma Death a
comb for her lank locks and would fear-
lessly have stroked her fleshless shoulder
saying gently "Why Mrs. Bones, my dear,
haven't you come a little early?"
I think you would not have withheld
even from Death's self your thou-ing
greeting once you beheld
that incurable at your elbow.
You fought to keep her waiting for
you in the hallway while she
scratched and finally pounded on your door
but once she entered and that door closed
behind her you recognized the fact
of her outrageous presence and the
courtesy and courage of your heart listened intact
to her untimely undeniable demand.

It is not easy to remember that you died.
Neither your funeral nor our tears persuade
us, yet, that you have died. We shall confide
to you in phantasy through years of need
the flabby failure, shabby sin, and pride-
fully, the high Hungarian deed.
Our spirits shall by your quick soul be fed
until our bodies, too, are dead.

IN MEMORY OF LEMUEL AYERS, SCENE DESIGNER,
Dead of Cancer in His Fortieth Year.

It is generall
To be mortall
I have well espied
No man may him hide
from death hollow-eyed.

John Skelton

I that indulgently
am still allowed to be
address these lines to the
"Late Lemuel Ayers" who
did not elect to do
his dying young

Lem you are early late
your life and death complete,
somewhere our dyings wait.
Finished with and by pain
you will not feel again
forgive us grief

Magical from the start
your strict and dazzling art
pure as your eye's taut heart
delicate bold and rare
castled the empty air
splendoring space

Truth-vizored knight of risk
vulnerable in your casque
magician of the masque
sword-wand in hand you strove
to conquer goat-foot's grove,
laurel your crown

Raped of felicity
ambushed unknowingly
by your bones' treachery
outraged by cone and knife
you labored for your life,
Myrtle, your wreath

Now you indulgently
observe our boon to be
alive and grieved, but the
shame is you've few friends who
dare to expect to do
their dying old.

ON LOOKING IN THE LOOKING GLASS

Your small embattled eyes dispute a face
that middle-aging sags and creases.
Besieged, your eyes protest and plead,
your wild little eyes are bright, and bleed.

And now in an instant's blink my stare
seizes in your beleaguered glare
the pristine gaze the blown-glass stance
of your once
total innocence.
I see and dare the child you were.

And for a wink's lasting, There
Now in your blistered eyes dazzles the flare
of Youth with years and love to swear
the kindling enkindled fire
heedless and sheer . . .
I see and fear the girl you were.

And now for a tic's lending, Now for the stint
of a second's fission I light to the glint
of your Daemon, that familiar whom you stint
so prodigally. Shunting, shan't-
ing, wincing fabricant
I see the maker that you want
and aren't.

And now just now I closed your eyes
your infant ancient naked eyes.
Gaze glare and flare and glint are buried by
my neutral eye-
lids. These island citadels are now surrendered
and with imagination's eye I see you dead.

"... AND THOU NO BREATH AT ALL?"

for Barbara Ransom Jopson, 1915–1957

Yours, Barbara, was a literal way of death.
You were defaulted by the failure of your breath.
To fox the taxing of your faltering breath
you schooled yourself for years to snare
a reasonable surety of air . . .
not surplus air to waltz or to embrace
just marginal sips to stay, with grace,
alight, and spark the hovering dark of death
with bright unwavering speech. You flogged your breath
down your dogged days and spent that wilting breath
in dialogues that burnished us with your
ungarnishable gold where we before
had counterfeited in our brass or gilt. Your art
was alchemy wrought by a sleight of heart.
That art will lend us gold beyond your death
and round the bend of our last breath
when we like you end, as we must, all out of breath.

SALOON SUITE

I. *Accordion and Harmonica*
(Accordion)   *Waltz*

The red balloon will collapse, my sweet
The snowman will melt in the sun
The daffodil dries on the hill
              AND
the kite blows away out of sight
But the hurdy the gurdy still giddies the street
            and lilacs are BLOO-
               ming in Kew
and the dancing   the dancing
the rhyming romancing
will never no never be done.

(Harmonica)   *Jig*

Murphy and company jig with Cohen
Shicker vie a Goy
Sing your slainthe landsmen
Lhude sing Lochheim
Joy and joy and joy
AND
Paesani   Please   It's time

NOTE.—This poem was written after hearing the "Third Man Theme," which should be kept in mind while reading Part II. "Shicker vie a Goy" is Yiddish for "drunk like a gentile," "Slainthe" is the Gaelic equivalent of "Here's to you," and "Lochheim" is Yiddish for "slainthe." "Landsmen" is Yiddish for "fellow townsmen."

SALOON SUITE

II. *Zither*   *Tango*

Loving you   Love   loving you
the least leaf
the least last lone-est leaf
redder is, red red   is redder
redder than   that maple grove
in fall   in fall in fall
                              and in
and in the spring   in the spring
the youngest and the littlest leaf
                    is green
a greener green a greenest green ah greener than
a willow tree
                    in May
in May in May
I love you, love you love   you far-
ther, than the farthest foam in
furthest most for ever wake of   sea-
lost shallop
and more particularly Love,   than
the look! look looked-for shell than
the sought-found-shell than
the small and the whole shell's
sweet scallop.
Lost   love-lost   love-lost
I am lost Love I am lost love-lost
Love lost.
Sail me sail me home
Sail me sail me sail me home
My sailor   sail me sail me home
Reef me   steer me. Navigate me
home   home   home   home
home.

LITTLE ROCK ARKANSAS 1957

dedicated to the nine children

Clasping like bucklers to their bodies, books,
nine children move through blasts of killing looks.
Committed to this battle each child dares,
deliberately, the fusillades of jeers.
Their valor iron in their ironed clothes
they walk politely in their polished shoes
down ambushed halls to classrooms sown with mines
to learn their lesson. Obviously nine's
a carefully calculated number, odd
not even, a suave size that can be add-
ed to, discreetly, later, or culled now
should one child break not bend; or fail to bow
sufficiently his bloody head . . . a rule
to heed, child, be you black and going to school.

LETTER FROM SLOUGH POND

Here where you left me alone
the soft wind sighs through my wishbone
the sun is lapping at my flesh
I couple with the ripples of the fresh
pond water I am rolled by the roiling sea.
Love, in our wide bed, do you lie lonely?
The spoon of longing stirs my marrow
and I thank God this bed is narrow.

THE SEARCHLIGHT

From an anti-aircraft battery

In smug delight we swaggered through the park
and arrogant pressed arm and knee and thigh.
We could not see the others in the dark.
We stopped and peered up at the moonless sky
and at grey bushes and the bristling grass
You in your Sunday suit, I in my pleated gown,
deliberately we stooped (brim-full of grace,
each brandied each rare-steaked) and laid us down.

We lay together in that urban grove
an ocean from the men engaged to die.
As we embraced a distant armoured eye
aroused our dusk with purposed light, a grave
rehearsal for another night. The field
bloomed lovers, dined and blind and target-heeled.

MATHEMATICS OF ENCOUNTER

Two never-ever-will-be lovers each
thatched in a thicket of one-
liness, huddled in onlyhood,
reach eye to perilous eye and contract
in an absolute gaze, in a clasping
of I's, a wedding. In that (ah marginal)
marrying of marrows, flesh blooms and bells,
blood shimmers and arrows, bones melt
and meld, loins lock.
In that look's-lasting love is resolved
to one-plus-one, dissolved again to two, these
    two absolved,
and the equation solved.

MEA CULPA

I do not love thee, Doctor Fell
The reason why I cannot tell
But this one thing I know full well
I do not love thee, Dr. Fell

The plane rose loudly and rammed west
while I, as usual afraid, rejoiced
that the stranger beside me hid
the window's terrible view of our toy
enormous tinkered wing tilting
and shuddering out there
in the middle of the air.

I looked at the man by my side
and saw one eye, cheek, ear, and hearing aid.
His tears fell out the eye and down the cheek.
Turning his head he fused his spilling gaze
to mine and begging angrily he said
"I am a surgeon hired to patch
the almost dead alive
but Doctor Fell will not arrive.

He is expected; and further
he is expected by the families
of the dying, who pay his monstrous fee
and fare, to be God Almighty's cousin . . .
whereas, clearly, I am not even
on time, lady, not even perhaps in
time, because a flight was cancelled." Knowing
him deaf I loudly cried
him grace, yelling, "You tried . . .
and they will know that you tried."

He mentioned trains and that they run on time
and that perhaps the waiting dying man
had died. "Yes, I am a surgeon," he said
softly, "but I had rather peddle used
cars to buy my beer. I am tired I
am tired of this frightful trust when I
confront and cut a bleeding carcass."
Touching his hand I blared
that the very FACT that he cared . . .

"Care, care," he said as tears still slid
from his eyes, "can't you see I am not there?"
Abruptly he pulled a silver pill-box
from his pocket, and showing me his hands
and how they shook, he said, "I take a pill
at intervals to make my hands belong
and if I time the taking perfectly
these hands behave; they are golden, lady,
not one qualm or quiver in these
fingers, in these wrists, this heart,
or any other part."

I thought but could not bellow, yes, you care,
but the choice was yours; you made it leniently.
Your tears and pills and knives, my glib compassion
and my cadenced cant, these bleeding hearts
that blossom on our sleeves will not enlarge the
spirit, Doctor, nor reduce the spleen. We
must commit the act of caring before
indulging in elegiac tears. Our bills and
visits must be paid, our letters written,
our departures and arrivals made on time.
Trusting your weather eye
you assumed that plane would fly.

"Please forgive me that I have no comfort
for you". . . . I spoke out loud, but, not, it seemed,
quite loud enough, for he paid no heed, and
kneading his hands, remained silent until
our plane landed. I wished then to will him
well, but under the circumstances,
a resonant Good Luck struck me as flippant,
and a shouted Good-bye redundant.

SUMMER REMEMBERED

Sounds sum and summon the remembering of summers.
The humming of the sun
The mumbling in the honey-suckle vine
The whirring in the clovered grass
The pizzicato plinkle of ice in an auburn
uncle's amber glass.
The whing of father's racquet and the whack
of brother's bat on cousin's ball
and calling voices call-
ing voices spilling voices . . .

The munching of saltwater at the splintered dock
The slap and slop of waves on little sloops
The quarreling of oarlocks hours across the bay
The canvas sails that bleat as they
are blown. The heaving buoy bell-
ing HERE I am
HERE you are HEAR HEAR

listen listen listen
The gramophone is wound
the music goes round and around
BYE   BYE BLUES   LINDY'S COMING
voices calling   calling   calling
"Children!   Children!   Time's Up
Time's Up"
Merrily sturdily wantonly the familial voices
cheerily chidingly call to the children   TIME'S UP
and the mute children's unvoiced clamor sacks the summer air
crying Mother   Mother   are you there?

PART OF THE DARKNESS

I had thought of the bear in his lair as fiercely free, feasting
    on honey and wildwood fruits;

I had imagined a forest lunge, regretting the circus shuffle and
    the zoo's proscribed pursuits.

Last summer I took books and children to Wisconsin's Great
    North woods. We drove

one night through miles of pines and rainy darkness to a garbage
    grove

that burgeoned broken crates and bulging paper bags and emptied
    cans of beer,

to watch for native bears, who local guides had told us, scavenged
    there.

After parking behind three other cars (leaving our headlights on
    but dim)

We stumbled over soggy moss to join the families blinking on
    the rim

of mounded refuse bounded east north and west by the forest.

The parents hushed and warned their pushing children each of
    whom struggled to stand nearest

the arena, and presently part of the darkness humped away from
    the foliage and lumbered bear-shaped

toward the heaping spoilage. It trundled into the litter while we
    gaped,

and for an instant it gaped too, bear-faced, but not a tooth was
  bared. It grovelled

carefully while tin cans clattered and tense tourists tittered. Pains-
  takingly it nosed and ravelled

rinds and husks and parings, the used and the refused; bear-
  skinned and doggedly explored

the second-hand remains while headlights glared and flashlights
  stared and shamed bored

children booed, wishing aloud that it would trudge away so they
  might read its tracks.

They hoped to find an as yet unclassified spoor, certain that no
  authentic bear would turn his back

upon the delicacies of his own domain to flounder where mere
  housewives' leavings rot.

I also was reluctant to concede that there is no wild honey in the
  forest and no forest in the bear.

Bereaved, we started home, leaving that animal there.

AT A SUMMER HOTEL

I am here with my beautiful bountiful womanful child
to be soothed by the sea not roused by these roses roving wild.
My girl is gold in the sun and bold in the dazzling water,
she drowses on the blond sand and in the daisy fields my daughter
dreams. Uneasy in the drafty shade I rock on the verandah
reminded of Europa Persephone Miranda.

A LOUD SONG, MOTHER

My son is five years old and tonight he sang this song to me.
He said, it's a loud song, Mother, block up your ears a little, he
said wait I must get my voice ready first. Then tunelessly
but with a bursting beat he chanted from his room enormously,
>strangers in my name
>strangers all around me
>strangers running toward me
>strangers all over the world
>strangers running on stars
A deafening declaration this jubilant shout of grief
that trumpets final fellowship and flutes a whole belief.
Alone and in the dark he clears his throat to yawp his truth
that each living human creature's name is Ruth.
He sings a world of strangers running on the burning stars
a race on every-colored feet with freshly calloused scars.

Our stark still strangers waited back of doors and under beds
their socket eyes stared at us out of closets; in our heads.
We crawled on hob-nailed knees across our wasted starless land
each smugly thinking his the only face that wore a brand.

Sons, may you starve the maggot fears that ate our spirit's meat
and stride with brother strangers in your seven-league bare feet.

THAT PRINCELING

"Here is a candle to light you to bed
here comes the chopper to chop off your head"

That princeling bland with dapper smiles for daylit danger,
that dauphin gay as a dolphin at high noon,
in the purring night, pawed by the furry darkness,
howls mutely at the looming loneliness.

In his cold comfortable cage (unguarded)
bulging with beasts, pulsing with strangers,
in a ferocity of silence, it is his own
soft breath that pads and pants and pauses.

Bereaved and unbelieved, beset, be-nighted,
wincing from the awaited and insupportable pounce,
his little tender burrowing bones
bury him to bed.
     No lance no bow of burning gold
     No ewe no shepherd and no fold
     No jerkin of green nor coat of mail, no grace nor grail
     Can celebrate or succour him. Fearful and frail
that trembling desolate and dear prince cringes on his cot
while down unending corridors behind an arras (innocent and not
unarrogant with unicorns) the dauntless King and Queen
waltz sumptuously to sleep.

CANZONETTA

for a god-son aged five

Swim little king-fish Leap small salmon
Sally from the sea and up the stream Fling
Game as Isaac and gold as Mammon
Plunge April fishlet Sprintheart dash
Drought's the drowning though love is rash
And anglers bait to poach your dreaming
    Cheat that larder, Beat that Chowder, Splash!

Gambol Gamble Easter lambling
Adam as Ram and mortal as Mother
Baa your benison Ding your damning
Bruise and blessing bell your bleating
Carillon lambkin rousing routing no retreating
Hurtle into wolf and spring's bell-wether
Spiel your glock and, spell your flock, and Ring!

Gallivant giddyap bantam Will-joy
Bold as bugle and brave as bunting
Trumpet! Furl out! Bannering boy
Gallop to the hill-top. Strut your stride
Raising praising choosing losing never hide-
ing, heeled by the hope that hounds your hunting
    Sound your horn Astound your dawn and Ride

NOT AT ALL WHAT ONE IS USED TO ...

There was never any worry about bread or even butter
although that worried me almost as much as my stutter.
I drank coffee with the others in drugstores and then went
back to my room for which I paid a lower rent
than I could afford and where I was proud
of the bedbugs, and where I often allowed
myself an inadequate little Rhine wine. Two
or three times a week after seeing the producers who
were said to be looking for comedy types I wandered
off to the movies alone and always wondered
if anyone in the mezzanine knew me by sight, or might
know me by name or have kissed me and I felt an itch
to stand right up and ask, like swearing out loud in church.
Only one agent agreed to be rude to me every day, a
cross cockeyed woman who had acted in her youth.
I was not union because I had never been paid and the truth
is no other agent would speak to me or even see me until I was
    Equity . . .
a vicious circle but not unpleasing to me.
I smoked for hours in producers' anterooms where
I prayed that interviews I had come there
to beseech would be denied.
Usually my prayers were granted and I stayed outside.
I was a tense imposter, a deliberate dunce,
in a lobby of honest earnest seekers. Once
or twice thanks to a letter of introduction I
got to see the man, but instead of "chin up" and "do or die"
I effectively slouched and stammered in disorder in order
to thus escape the chance to read I might be
offered. An English director once said I was the
"perfect adorable silly ass," due in part to a part
he saw me do in which I had to lisp and giggle.

But that of course was in another country. I did not boggle
at summer stock, and somewhere north of Boston I had
at last become a paid member of a company where sad
to relate I was successfully grotesque in numerous unglamourous
bit parts (usually dialect for I did not stutter
in dialect) and I was always differently grotesque, utter-
ly; but people laughed and/or cried, always saying I was playing myself, that I was a 'natural'. Through the good offices of a
well-connected friend I at last read for a producer who was
    Broadway
and was given the part of a Cockney maid, afraid
and eager, who moved and talked in double-time.
But I was fired. The stars complained for no rime
or reason that they became confused when I was 'on' (there was
    no basis
for their saying that the audience laughed too much and in the
    wrong places)
although it is possible that I just did everything faster and faster.
I had come to depend on the laughs and dismissal was a disaster.
My next job was a haughty lady's maid with a faint brogue
and a strip-tease walk. One night (in Hartford) I was more rogue-
ish than usual and the college boys broke up the show
banging their feet on the floor and whistling. Not long ago
I portrayed a madwoman (but gentle and sentimental)
I curtseyed, sang a short song as I did not
stammer when I sang, and fondled a telescope that
had belonged to a sea-going ancestor. It was agreed
that at last, despite previous successes, I had indeed
and finally found my niche. It was declared
that I could go on and on doing that kind of thing, but I dared
myself to attempt only straight parts although it is hard (playing
    with fire)
for a character actress to play herself and only too true
that the audience response is not at all what one is used to.
Nevertheless it is a challenge and no reason to retire.

SUMMERS AGO

For Edith Sitwell

The Ferryman fairied us out to sea
Gold gold gold sang the apple-tree

Children I told you I tell you our sun was a hail of gold!
I say that sun stoned, that sun stormed our tranquil, our blue bay
bellsweet saltfresh water (bluer than tongue-can-tell, daughter)
and dazed us, darlings, and dazzled us, I say that sun crazed
(that sun clove) our serene as ceramic selves and our noon glazed
    cove,
and children all that grew wild by the wonderful water shot tall
as tomorrow, reeds suddenly shockingly green had sprouted like
    sorrow
and crimson explosions of roses arose in that flurry of Danaean
    glory
while at night we did swoon ah we swanned to a silverer moon-
    light than listen or lute,
we trysted in gondolas blown from glass and kissed in fluted
    Venetian bliss.

> Sister and brother I your mother
> Once was a girl in skirling weather
> Though summer and swan must alter, falter,
> I waltzed on the water once, son and daughter.

is one game that no-one quits while he or she's ahead. The
stakes are steep. Among the chips are love fame life and sanity.
The game's risk is that winning one chip often means the forfeit
of another but despite the penalties there is a surfeit
of players. Some are only kibbitzers, others play it safe
(their chips are counterfeit) cheating, they may not come to grief,
or so they hope, and hoping keep their places near the pot.
There are other gambits deployed to trick the croupier's hot
eye and hand. For some in terror for their reason and their rhyme
There's a disguise in style to rent or borrow or assume:
hair-shirts, brocaded waistcoats (the gilt is slightly tarnished)
sackcloth interlined, embroidered chasubles refurbished,
helmets turbans caps (with bells) wreaths high silk hats cockades . . .
and for women Quaker bonnets wimples coifs and sun-shades,
long blue stockings hawking gloves a fan a hobnailed boot.
But it's the gamblers wearing their own hides who shoot
the moon rocketing on unprotected feet to outer space
where (out of pocket, having no sleeves up which to hide an ace)
they fall bankrupt or being down to their last chip are stran-
ded. No-one has pocketed the moon since the game began . . .
or . . . sooner than they did
they died.

JEAN SANS TERRE
WRAPS HIMSELF IN A RED COAT

Coming toward you in my red coat
Do not ask me if I wear the mantle of the king of Tyre
Or the cloak of the beggar of Benares
My coat is lined with love

The song of love goes before me as crimson dust
Preceded the sirocco which trails the sulphurous storm
It breathes above the seven couching hills
Before astounding the valleys of thirst dried up by Satan

For it is a wind of anger that swells my bloody coat
And flares my pine torch from the forest's depths
I carry vengeance to the people who still dream
In the strangled slums, in the hangars of nightmare

In the flophouses of the Beggar's Court
In the bazaars where hang the carpets blood-stained
By the thousand-year-old hand of slaves
In the prisons cemented by tears and petrified skulls

I light I light with my dancing torch
The tarnished skies of the cities
For the poor who exist on the thirst of others
And have not the right to be thirsty

Those who peddle the song of apples
Of milk of rain of air and the coca of the Trusts
Those who sell exactly enough to die,
To dress the abscessed wounds of their children

I come I come on my red horse
Whose wings are put together with flaps
Torn in strips from my heart, from my vagabond's coat . . .
His hooves flower the rock to a rosebush of love

His nostrils breathe fire from the stars to you
I come from the depths of the forever virgin forest
And I kindle for you all the birds of my crown
The fire of the lyre-bird and the golden fire of the phoenix

A universal Saint Elmo's fire
To spark men's dust
To portion joy to all the corners of the world
To wrap you, my brothers, in a crimson coat

JEAN SANS TERRE
THE CHEST OF DRAWERS

I am a chest of drawers
Open to the passerby
Containing enough to eat and drink
And above all to die

Here is the bunch of mouldering keys
The bouquet of keys to fields and dreams
Here is the key which locks the door of grace
And the one which will open my tomb again

In this drawer I have the essence of rain
And the spices of the earth
Pepper for killing memories
And shadow—dissolving salt.

In another a gold ancestral watch
The watch time cannot break
Anger Love Nothing stops it
No hammer shatters this dial

Here is the keen edge to sever trust
The wool for mending friendship
But alas I have dropped the stitch
Which could re-weave the wing of innocence

The pack of cards from which my wife emerged
The accountings which prolong the lunar year
And my will written in invisible ink
Will see the notaries of Tartar age.

This compass measures the angle of sincerity
And this bell pings for every lie
And here is a life-supply of nails
To crucify the guilty.

There I have the bleached heart of my mother
Who always knitted socks for the condemned
And I have the ivory hand of my love
Lost as she leant to wave farewell

The seventh drawer contains the tools of prayer
The gimlet for the worm of temptation
The file against the growth of impoverished thoughts
And the pliers to screw tight the piety of my hands

> I am a chest of drawers
> Locked from the passerby
> Containing enough to doubt and trust
> And above all to die